Bake
- a -
Cake

Contents

Perfect Puddings

Delicious Drinks

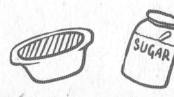

Introduction

Welcome to *Bake-a-Cake*! In this book you'll find tons of delicious recipes that are all super easy and enjoyable to make. Whether you want to bake fairy cakes for a sleepover, flapjacks for afternoon tea with your family or whip up a fruit smoothie for Saturday breakfast, there are recipes to suit every occasion.

Baking is so much fun – plus at the end you get something delicious to share with your family and friends.

Here are some top tips for getting started:
- Make sure you've told an adult that you're planning to cook, and that you've got time to prepare and bake it.
- Put on an apron (things can get messy!), tie long hair back and wash your hands.
- Read the recipe all the way through before you start.
- Weigh out all the ingredients and lay out any equipment you'll need. That way you won't get halfway through and realise you're missing something important!

And don't forget to clear up afterwards. It's not as fun as baking, but it has to be done!

Are you ready to create something yummy? Let's get baking!

Warning! Make sure you ask an adult to help you whenever you'd like to use the hob or the oven. And always wear oven gloves when you're holding hot trays or pans.

Useful Equipment

Here's a quick guide to the equipment that you'll need most often for the recipes in this book.

measuring scales and
  measuring jug
20cm round cake tin
35 x 25cm rectangular cake tin
20 x 20cm square cake tin
12-hole cupcake/muffin tin
large loaf tin
large ovenproof dish
baking tray
wire rack

variety of mixing bowls (at
  least one big and two small)
blender
cookie cutters (variety of sizes
  and shapes)
essential utensils: wooden
  spoons, whisk, sieve, grater,
  palette knife, pastry brush,
  rolling pin, measuring spoons
greaseproof paper

Conversion Chart

Use this handy chart if you need to convert the UK baking measurements to US measurements.

	1 cup	3/4 cup	2/3 cup	1/2 cup	1/3 cup	1/4 cup	1 tbsp	1 tsp
FLOUR	125g	95g	85g	65g	40g	30g	8g	-
WHITE SUGAR	200g	150g	135g	100g	70g	50g	13g	-
BROWN SUGAR	180g	135g	120g	90g	60g	45g	12g	-
BUTTER/ MARGARINE	225g	180g	150g	110g	75g	60g	13g	-
OATS	85g	60g	60g	45g	30g	20g	5g	-
CHOPPED NUTS/ RAISINS/SULTANAS	150g	115g	110g	75g	50g	40g	10g	-
HONEY/ TREACLE/ SYRUP	340g	250g	225g	170g	110g	85g	22g	7g
MILK/CREAM/ WATER					75ml	60ml	15ml	5ml

Fabulous Fairy Cakes

Fairy cakes are just like their American friends –
cupcakes – but smaller and even easier to make.

Ingredients

265g butter, room temperature
115g caster sugar
2 eggs, beaten
1 tbsp milk
1 tsp vanilla essence
115g self-raising flour
½ tsp baking powder
300g icing sugar
2 tbsp milk

Equipment

3 bowls – 1 small, 2 large
fork, to beat the eggs
wooden spoon
whisk
2 x 12-hole bun tins
paper cases
teaspoon
wire rack
table knife

1. Ask an adult to preheat the oven to 180°C/350°F/gas mark 4.

2. Put 115g of your butter and all of the caster sugar into a large bowl. Mix with a wooden spoon until the mixture is light and fluffy.

3. Add the beaten eggs, milk and vanilla essence. Whisk together.

4. Add the flour and baking powder and whisk together until you have a smooth mixture.

5. Fill two 12-hole bun tins with paper cupcake cases. Use a teaspoon to half fill each of the cases with your mixture.

6. Ask an adult to put your fairy cakes into the oven for 10 minutes and leave to cool on a wire rack.

7. For the buttercream icing, put the rest of the butter (150g) into a large bowl and beat with a wooden spoon until it is light, fluffy and a pale yellow colour.

8. Add 150g of the icing sugar and stir until it is all mixed in. Then add the rest of the icing sugar and mix together again.

9. Stir in the milk a little at a time until you have a smooth mixture.

TIP:
Make your fairy cakes extra special by adding food colouring to your icing and putting sprinkles on top.

10. Use a table knife to carefully cut a circle off the top of each of your cakes, creating a small hole. Put the spare pieces of cake to one side and fill the holes with a dollop of icing.

11. Using a table knife, cut each the spare piece of cake in half and push the two halves into the icing, so they look like wings.

Victoria Sponge

When you taste your jam-filled creation,
you won't believe how easy it is to make.

Ingredients

200g butter, room temperature,
plus extra for greasing
200g caster sugar
1 tsp vanilla extract
4 eggs, beaten
200g self-raising flour
1 tsp baking powder
5 tbsp strawberry jam
2 tbsp icing sugar

Equipment

2 bowls – 1 small, 1 large
fork, to beat the eggs
2 x 20cm round cake tins
greaseproof paper
pencil
scissors
wooden spoon
sieve
wire rack

1. Ask an adult to preheat your oven to 190°C/375°F/gas mark 5.

2. Use kitchen paper to grease your two cake tins with butter.

3. Fold a piece of greaseproof paper in half and place one of
   the cake tins on top. Draw around the tin with a pencil and
   cut out your circle. You will be left with two circles. Pop one
   onto the base of each tin.

4. Cream together your butter, sugar and vanilla extract by
   mixing them with a wooden spoon in a large bowl, until the
   mixture is light and fluffy.

5. Beat the eggs into the mixture.

6. Next, sieve in the flour and baking powder and fold it into the mixture by going all the way around the edge of the bowl once and then 'folding' the mixture on top of itself into the middle of the bowl. Repeat until all of the flour is mixed in.

TIP:
To make the filling even more delicious, you could add a layer of whipped cream before you spread over the jam.

7. Spoon half of the mixture into each tin and spread so it covers the base of the tin evenly.

8. Ask an adult to put your tins into the oven for 20 minutes until they are a golden-yellow colour.

9. Remove your cakes from the tins and place them on a wire rack until cool.

10. Spread the top of one of your cakes with jam and place the other cake on top.

11. Sprinkle the top with icing sugar and enjoy!

Tottenham Cake

Squares of Tottenham cake used to be sold for a penny each! They are utterly delicious no matter which football team you support.

Ingredients

225g butter, room temperature, plus extra for greasing
225g caster sugar
4 eggs, beaten
280g self-raising flour
2½ tsp baking powder
2 tsp lemon zest, grated
4 tbsp milk
300g icing sugar
5–6 tbsp water
1 drop pink food colouring

Equipment

3 bowls – 2 small, 1 large
fork, to beat the eggs
grater, for the zest
35 x 25cm rectangular cake ti
kitchen paper
greaseproof paper
scissors
2 spoons – 1 wooden, 1 metal
wire rack
palette knife
table knife

1. Ask an adult to preheat your oven to 180°C/350°F/gas mark 4.

2. Use kitchen paper to grease the inside of a cake tin with butter. Line it with greaseproof paper.

3. Fold a piece of greaseproof paper in half and place one of the cake tins on top. Draw around the tin with a pencil and cut out your circle. You will be left with two circles. Pop one onto the base of each tin.

4. Cream together the butter and sugar in a large bowl, mixing them with a wooden spoon until the mixture is light and fluffy.

5. Add the flour and baking powder. Fold them into the mixture by going all the way around the edge of the bowl once and then 'folding' the mixture on top of itself into the middle of the bowl. Repeat until all of the flour is mixed in.

6. Finally, add the lemon zest and milk and stir well.

7. Spoon the mix into your tin. Smooth it out with a metal spoon.

8. Ask an adult to put the tin into the oven for 35 minutes, or until golden. Remove from the oven and leave on a wire rack to cool.

9. For the icing, put your icing sugar into a small bowl and add a little water at a time, until you have a smooth runny paste. Add the food colouring and stir until you have an even pink colour.

10. Once the cake is cool, turn it the right way up and pour the icing over your cake. Spread it evenly over the top and sides using a palette knife. Leave to set.

11. Cut your cake into squares using a table knife and enjoy while watching the football.

Bara Brith

This traditional Welsh recipe actually has tea inside the cake! Tea and cake in one mouthful – delicious.

Ingredients

225g mixed dried fruit
400ml strong, hot tea, no milk
knob of butter
175g self-raising flour
175g wholemeal flour
1 tsp baking powder
1½ tsp mixed spice
60g soft brown sugar
1 egg, beaten

Equipment

3 bowls – 1 small, 2 large
fork, to beat the egg
teapot
large loaf tin
kitchen paper
wooden spoon
wire rack

1. Put the dried fruit in a bowl and pour over the hot tea. Stir together and leave the fruit to soak overnight.

2. Ask an adult to preheat the oven to 160°C/320°F/gas mark 3.

3. Use kitchen paper to grease the inside of a loaf tin with butter.

4. Tip both flours, the baking powder, spice and sugar into a large bowl and stir together.

5. Pour in the beaten egg and the fruit, along with any tea still in the bowl. Mix together until the fruit is evenly spread in the mixture.

6. Spoon your mixture into the loaf tin. Squash it into the corners and smooth on the top.

7. Ask an adult to put your cake in the oven for 1 hour and 20 minutes and then leave to cool for 10 minutes.

8. Remove your loaf from the tin and place on a wire rack to cool.

9. Cut up your loaf, spread the slices with butter and enjoy with more tea.

Teatime Treats

Welsh Cakes

These are a delicious teatime treat, traditionally called 'pice ar y maen' in Welsh.

Ingredients

225g plain flour, plus extra
  for dusting
85g caster sugar
1 tsp mixed spice
1 tsp baking powder
¼ tsp salt
105g butter, cut into cubes
50g currants
1 egg, beaten
a little milk

Equipment

table knife, to cube the butter
2 bowls – 1 small, 1 large
fork, to beat the egg
rolling pin
7cm circular cutter
frying pan
fish slice
kitchen paper

1. Put the flour, sugar, spice, baking powder, salt and 100g of the butter into a large bowl.

2. Use your fingertips to rub the butter into the dry ingredients. Keep rubbing until all the big lumps have gone and the bowl looks like it is full of crumbs.

3. Add the currants and stir in the beaten egg until you get a stiff dough that you can squash together with your hands. If your mix looks too crumbly, add a little milk. If it's a bit sticky, add some more flour.

4. Sprinkle some flour onto your work surface and rolling pin and roll out your dough until it is 1.5cm thick. Add a splash more milk if your dough starts to dry out too much.

5. Use a 7cm circular cutter to cut circles out of your dough. Squash together any leftover dough and roll it out again. Cut as many circles as you can so there's no wasted dough.

6. Ask an adult to melt the rest of your butter (5g) in a frying pan over a low heat.

7. Ask an adult to add your cakes to the pan and fry for 3–4 minutes on each side. Carefully scoop them out with a fish slice and leave them to cool on kitchen paper.

8. Serve your cakes with butter and lots of yummy jam!

Hot Cross Buns

Nothing says springtime more than hot cross buns!

Ingredients

50g butter, plus extra for
  greasing
200ml milk
500g strong white bread flour
3 tsp mixed spice
50g caster sugar
7g sachet of fast-action yeast
pinch of salt
2 eggs, beaten
200g currants
75g plain flour, plus extra for dusting
4 tbsp water
1 tbsp golden syrup

Equipment

3 bowls – 2 small, 1 large
fork, to beat the egg
large baking tray
kitchen paper
saucepan
wooden spoon
2 tea towels
sandwich bag
pastry brush

1. Use kitchen paper to grease a large baking tray with butter.

2. Ask an adult to bring the milk to the boil in a saucepan, then remove it from the heat. Add the butter and stir until it melts. Leave to cool for 10 minutes.

3. Mix the strong white bread flour, spice, sugar, yeast and salt together in a large bowl. Pour in the warm milk and butter mixture. Add the beaten eggs and stir until you have a sticky dough.

4. Sprinkle the spare flour onto your work surface and put the dough on top of it. Knead the dough by squashing and squeezing it between your hands and against the work surface for 10 minutes, until it is smooth and squashy.

5. Put the dough back into your bowl and cover with a tea towel. Leave in a warm place for 1 hour.

6. Take the tea towel off the bowl. The dough should have doubled in size.

7. Tip in your currants and knead the dough again until the fruit is all mixed in.

8. Split your dough into 12 equal pieces and shape them into balls by rolling them between your palms. Place the balls of dough onto your baking tray, 5cm apart. Cover with a clean tea towel and leave in a warm place for 1 hour.

9. Ask an adult to preheat the oven to 220°C/425°F/gas mark 7.

10. For the icing, mix the plain flour and the water in a small bowl and spoon into a sandwich bag. Carefully snip a small corner off the bag and gently squeeze two lines of flour paste onto the top of each bun to make a cross.

11. Ask an adult to pop your buns into the oven for 15 minutes, or until golden brown.

12. Brush with golden syrup and then leave to cool for 10 minutes. Split in half, spread with butter and enjoy.

Fat Rascals

These Yorkshire scones date back to
Elizabethan times.

Ingredients

300g self-raising flour, plus
  extra for dusting
½ tsp baking powder
130g butter, cut into cubes
100g caster sugar
1 tsp mixed spice
150g mixed dried fruit
zest of 1 orange, grated
zest of 1 lemon, grated
50ml double cream
2 eggs, beaten
50g glacé cherries, halved
25g flaked almonds

Equipment

table knife, to cube the butter
  and halve the cherries
2 bowls – 1 small, 1 large
fork, to beat the eggs
grater, for the zests
large baking tray
greaseproof paper
wooden spoon
rolling pin
pastry brush

1. Ask an adult to preheat the oven to 200°C/400°F/gas mark 6.

2. Take a large baking tray and line it with greaseproof paper.

3. Mix the flour and baking powder in a large bowl. Add the butter and use your fingertips to rub in the butter until your bowl looks like it is filled with crumbs.

4. Add the sugar, spice, dried fruit and zests, and stir together.

5. Add the cream and half of the egg mixture, and stir until you have a soft dough.

6. Dust your surface with flour and roll out the dough until it's 2.5cm thick. Divide the dough into six pieces, shape into rounds and put them on the baking tray.

7. Brush each bun with the remaining egg. Press a cherry and almonds into the top of each bun.

8. Ask an adult to put them into the oven for 15 minutes until golden and then leave to cool.

9. Slice them in half and spread with clotted cream and strawberry jam. Yum!

Cornish Saffron Buns

Saffron can be very expensive, but you only need to use a little pinch to make these yummy yellow buns.

Ingredients

pinch of saffron
1 tbsp hot water
125g butter, cut into cubes, plus extra for greasing
600g white bread flour, plus extra for dusting
pinch of salt
7g sachet of fast-action yeast
80g caster sugar
150ml milk
1 egg, beaten
100ml water
175g currants

Equipment

table knife, to cube the butter
3 bowls – 1 small, 2 large
fork, to beat the egg
egg cup
2 large baking trays
kitchen paper
wooden spoon
cling film
wire rack

1. Put the saffron in an egg cup and ask an adult to add the hot water. Leave to stand for 15 minutes.

2. Use kitchen paper to grease two large baking trays with butter.

3. Mix the flour and salt together in a large bowl. Add the cubed butter and use your fingertips to rub it in until your bowl looks like it is filled with crumbs.

4. Add the yeast, sugar and saffron water and mix well.

5. Pour the milk into a saucepan and ask an adult to slowly warm it on the hob.

6. In another large bowl, mix the beaten egg, warm milk and water and then pour it into the flour mixture. Stir together until you have a sticky dough.

7. Sprinkle the spare flour onto your surface and knead the dough for 5 minutes until it is stretchy and smooth.

8. Add the currants and squash them into the dough until they are all mixed in.

9. Break your dough into 12 and shape each piece into a ball.

10. Place the balls onto the baking trays, 5cm apart, and cover loosely with cling film.

11. Leave in a warm place for 45 minutes. They should have doubled in size.

12. Ask an adult to preheat the oven to 220°C/425°F/gas mark 7.

13. Ask an adult to put your buns into the oven for 20 minutes and then leave them to cool on a wire rack.

Scottish Macaroons

Make these and you will never look at a spud in the same way.

Ingredients

100g potatoes
2 tbsp butter
1 tbsp milk
3 drops vanilla essence
500g icing sugar
100g desiccated coconut
300g dark chocolate, in pieces

Equipment

potato peeler
table knife
2 saucepans
colander
20 x 20cm square cake tin
large baking tray
greaseproof paper
2 bowls – 1 small, 1 large
sieve
wooden spoon
greaseproof paper
a large plate

1. Carefully remove the skin of the potatoes with a peeler. Chop them in half with a table knife.

2. Put the potatoes into a saucepan and cover with water. Ask an adult to bring them to the boil, then simmer for 15–20 minutes until the potatoes are soft all the way through.

3. Drain the potatoes in a colander, then return to the pan and add the butter and milk, and mash until they are smooth with no lumps. Leave to cool.

4. Line a 20 x 20cm cake tin and a baking tray with greaseproof paper.

5. Put the mashed potato and vanilla essence into a large bowl. Sieve roughly one third of the icing sugar into the mixture. Stir until all the sugar is mixed in. Add another third and stir again. Add the rest of the icing sugar until you have a sticky paste.

6. Spoon the mix into the cake tin and spread into the corners. Put it into the freezer for 2 hours.

7. Ask an adult to heat the oven to 160°C/320°F/gas mark 3.

8. Sprinkle the coconut onto the baking tray. Ask an adult to put it into the oven for 3–4 minutes or until golden and leave to cool.

9. Ask an adult to bring a pan of water to the boil. Remove from the heat. Put the chocolate into a bowl and place the bowl on top of the pan. Leave it to stand for 5 minutes. Stir the chocolate to check it's all melted.

10. Take the potato mix out of the freezer and cut it into small bars using a table knife.

11. Ask an adult to help you dip each bar into the melted chocolate and then roll it in the coconut.

Mince Pies

Christmas wouldn't be Christmas without a warm mince pie. This year, why not try making your own?

Ingredients

a little flour, for dusting
300g shortcrust pastry
1 x 175g jar mincemeat
1 egg, beaten
1 tbsp icing sugar

Equipment

small bowl
fork, to beat the eggs
rolling pin
10cm circular cutter
12-hole bun tin
teaspoon
7cm circular cutter
pastry brush

1. Ask an adult to preheat your oven to 200°C/400°F/gas mark 6.

2. Sprinkle flour onto your work surface and rolling pin. Roll out your pastry until it is 3mm thick.

3. Use a 10cm circular cutter to cut out 12 pastry circles.

4. Place your pastry circles into a 12-hole bun tin, pressing each one gently into place.

5. Use a teaspoon to place a blob of mincemeat onto each circle.

6. Use a 7cm circular cutter to cut 12 lids from the rest of your pastry. Place a circle on top of each of your pies. Brush with egg.

7. Ask an adult to put them in the oven for 10–15 minutes.

8. Sprinkle with icing sugar and serve warm. Delicious!

TIP:
To make your mince pies look extra festive, use a star-shaped cutter to make the lids.

Biscuits & Sweets

Gingerbread People

It is said that the first gingerbread people were made for Elizabeth I, who asked her cooks to shape gingerbread to look like her favourite guests.

Ingredients

110g butter, cut into cubes, plus extra for greasing
350g plain flour, plus extra for dusting
6 tsp ground ginger
1 tsp bicarbonate of soda
175g soft brown sugar
5 tbsp golden syrup
1 egg, beaten
a few currants

Equipment

table knife, to cube the butter
2 bowls – 1 small, 1 large
fork, to beat the egg
2 large baking trays
kitchen paper
rolling pin
gingerbread man cutter

1. Ask an adult to preheat your oven to 180°C/350°F/gas mark 4.

2. Use kitchen paper to grease two large baking trays with butter.

3. Put the flour, ginger, bicarbonate of soda and butter in a large bowl. Rub the butter into the dry ingredients with your fingertips until the mixture looks like breadcrumbs.

4. Pour in the sugar, syrup and egg and squash it all together until you have a firm dough.

5. Dust your work surface and rolling pin with the spare flour. Roll out the dough until it is 5 mm thick.

6. Use a gingerbread man cutter to cut out as many people as you can from your dough.

7. Press together any leftover dough, roll it out again and cut out as many biscuits as you can, so there's no wasted dough.

8. Place your gingerbread people on your greased baking tray. Press two currants into the head of each of your people, for eyes.

9. Ask an adult to put your baking trays into the oven for 10–12 minutes until the biscuits are light brown and then leave to cool.

TIP:
Use icing and sweets to give your people some super-sweet outfits.

Chocolate-Chip Cookies

Wow your friends with these tasty treats.
They're super simple to make!

Ingredients

225g butter
100g caster sugar
200g brown sugar
1 tsp vanilla extract
2 eggs
350g plain flour
1 tsp bicarbonate of soda
1 tsp salt
350g chocolate chips (or any type
of chocolate crumbled up)

Equipment

large bowl
wooden spoon
2 large baking trays
wire rack (optional)

1. Ask an adult to preheat your oven to 190°C/375°F/gas mark 5.

2. In a large bowl, combine the butter, caster sugar, brown sugar and vanilla extract. Stir until this is light and fluffy, then beat the eggs.

3. Weigh out your flour into a medium-sized bowl and combine it with the bicarbonate of soda and salt. Then fold it into your sugar and butter mixture. Finally, add in your chocolate chips (or crumbled chocolate) and stir. You've now made your cookie dough!

4. Start taking small amounts of dough and rolling it into balls. Place the balls on two baking trays with lots of space between them. Bake them for 10–12 minutes, depending on how gooey you like them.

5. Leave them to cool on the baking trays (or on a wire rack), then share with friends. Delicious!

TIP: This recipe makes enough for approximately 12–15 cookies, depending on how big they are.

Shrewsbury Biscuits

These fruity biscuits come from Shrewsbury, in the West Midlands. They are mentioned in cookbooks as early as the 1650s.

Ingredients

125g butter, room temperature, plus extra for greasing
150g caster sugar
2 egg yolks
225g plain flour, plus extra for dusting
1 tbsp lemon zest, grated
75g currants

Equipment

grater, for the zest
2 large baking trays
kitchen paper
large bowl
wooden spoon
rolling pin
6cm circular fluted cutter

1. Ask an adult to preheat your oven to 180°C/350°F/gas mark 4.

2. Use kitchen paper to grease two large baking trays with butter.

3. Cream the butter and sugar together in a large bowl with a wooden spoon until the mixture is light and fluffy.

4. Add the egg yolks and stir until they are all mixed in.

5. Stir in the flour, lemon zest and currants until you have a crumbly dough that you can squash together with your hands.

6. Sprinkle flour onto your work surface and rolling pin and put the dough on top of it. Roll out the dough until it is 0.5cm thick.

7. Use your circular fluted cutter (one with crinkly edges) to cut out as many biscuits as you can from the dough.

8. Press together any leftover dough, then roll it out again and cut out more biscuits until you've used up all of the dough so there's none wasted.

9. Place the biscuits onto the baking trays and ask an adult to put them in the oven for 15 minutes, or until they are beginning to turn a pale golden colour.

10. Leave to cool and enjoy.

TIP:
If you store your biscuits in an air-tight container, like an old sweet tin or a Tupperware, they will last a lot longer.

Scottish Shortbread

It wouldn't be Christmas without some homemade treats. Try making this Scottish shortbread for everyone with a sweet tooth!

Ingredients

225g butter, plus extra
  for greasing
350g plain flour
100g caster sugar
pinch of salt

Equipment

greaseproof paper
large bowl
rolling pin
table knife
fork
wire rack

1. Ask an adult to preheat your oven to 170°C/325°F/gas mark 3.

2. Grease a baking tray with butter and line with greaseproof paper.

3. Sift the flour into a large bowl. Add the sugar, a pinch of salt and mix together.

4. Rub in the butter until the mixture is like breadcrumbs.

5. Knead the mixture well until it holds together, then gently roll it into a square, about 25 x 25cm and 2–3cm thick.

TIP:
Put your shortbread in a pretty box to make the perfect gift.

6. Carefully mark out slices with a knife and decorate by pricking with a fork.

7. Bake in the oven for 30–40 minutes, or until golden brown.

8. Ask an adult to help you remove it from the oven. Leave to cool on a wire rack and then dust with caster sugar.

Flapjacks

Chewy and oaty – perfect for walks in
the countryside.

Ingredients

300g butter, cut into cubes,
    plus extra for greasing
5 tbsp golden syrup
100g soft brown sugar
pinch of salt
500g rolled oats

Equipment

table knife, to cube the butter
rectangular cake tin
kitchen paper
large saucepan
wooden spoon

1. Ask an adult to preheat your oven to 180°C/350°F/gas mark 4.

2. Use kitchen paper to grease the inside of a cake tin with
   butter.

3. Ask an adult to slowly melt the remaining butter (300g) in a
   large saucepan.

4. Remove the saucepan from the heat. Add the syrup, sugar
   and salt and stir until all of the sugar has dissolved.

5. Add the oats and stir until they are coated with the sugary
   butter.

6. Spoon the mixture into the tin, pressing it into the corners and smoothing over the surface.

7. Ask an adult to put the tin into the oven for 25 minutes, or until the flapjack is golden.

8. Cut into rectangles using a table knife. Enjoy on a hike!

Chocolate Fudge

There are only four ingredients between you
and lip-lickingly good fudge.

Ingredients

500g chocolate, in pieces
60g butter, cut into cubes
1 tsp vanilla essence
1 x 397g can sweetened
  condensed milk

Equipment

20 x 20cm square cake tin
tin foil
scissors
saucepan

1. Cover the inside of a 20 x 20cm cake tin with foil.

2. Add the chocolate, butter and vanilla essence to a saucepan and pour in the condensed milk.

3. Ask an adult to put the pan over a low heat until all of the chocolate is melted. Stir well.

4. Pour the mixture into the cake tin and leave to cool. When cool, place in the fridge and leave to set for 3 hours.

5. Remove from the fridge and cut into pieces with a table knife.

TIP:
Take a pretty gift box, line it with tissue paper and pop in your fudge to make a sweet gift for a friend.

Chocolate Conkers

What better way to celebrate autumn than with a
heap of yummy chocolate conkers?

Ingredients

360g smooth peanut butter
1 tsp vanilla essence
120g butter, room temperature
400g icing sugar, sifted
300g dark chocolate, in pieces

Equipment

sieve, for the icing sugar
large baking tray
greaseproof paper
2 bowls – 1 small, 1 large
wooden spoon
tablespoon
saucepan
fork

1. Take a large baking tray and line it with greaseproof paper.

2. Mix the peanut butter, vanilla essence, butter and icing sugar
   in a bowl with a wooden spoon until it forms a thick dough.

3. Scoop out conker-sized lumps of dough using a tablespoon.
   Shape the lumps of dough into balls by rolling them between
   your palms.

4. Lay each ball on the baking tray and put the sheet into the
   fridge to chill for 1 hour.

5. To melt the chocolate, ask an adult to bring a pan of water to the boil and then remove it from the heat.

6. Put your chocolate pieces into a small bowl and place the bowl on top of the pan. Leave it to stand for 5 minutes. Give the chocolate a stir to check that it has completely melted.

7. Push a fork into a peanut-butter ball and dip the ball into the chocolate. Leave a small circle of the peanut-butter dough showing.

8. Pull your fork out and put the chocolate-covered ball back onto your baking tray, chocolate-side down. Repeat for the rest of your peanut-butter balls. Put them back in the fridge for 20 minutes to set.

9. Pile your conkers up and enjoy with a glass of cold milk.

Perfect Puddings

Eton Mess

This is one mess your parents will be happy
you made in the kitchen this summer.

Ingredients

400g strawberries
2 tsp caster sugar
500ml whipping cream
8 meringue nests

Equipment

table knife
colander
2 large bowls
whisk
metal spoon

1. Wash your strawberries in cold water. Cut off the stalks and cut the strawberries into quarters using a table knife. Put them in a bowl with the sugar.

2. In another bowl, whisk the cream until it can hold its shape on a spoon.

3. Crumble the meringue nests into the cream. Don't worry if the pieces are uneven, it all adds to the mess!

TIP:
Whisking cream can take some time so you may want to ask an adult's help, or use an electric whisk.

4. Add your strawberries and sugar and mix everything together with a metal spoon. Take care not to mix too hard so you don't break up the meringue more than you have to.

5. Serve in a large pretty bowl or in individual glasses.

Apple Crumble

This British pudding is easy to make and the perfect way to round off a traditional Sunday lunch.

Ingredients

100g caster sugar
225g butter, cut into cubes
210g plain flour
450g cooking apples, cut
  into 1.5cm chunks
75g soft brown sugar

Equipment

table knife, to cut the butter
  and apples
2 large bowls
wooden spoon
large ovenproof dish

1. Ask an adult to preheat the oven to 190°C/375°F/gas mark 5.

2. Put the caster sugar, butter and 200g of flour into a large bowl. Rub the butter into the mixture, using your fingertips, until you have no big lumps of butter left and the mixture looks like breadcrumbs.

3. Put your chunks of apple into another bowl. Stir together with the brown sugar and 10g of flour.

4. Tip your apple mix into a large ovenproof dish and cover evenly with your crumble topping from your first bowl.

5. Ask an adult to put the crumble into the oven for 1 hour until golden brown.

6. Leave to cool for 10 minutes before dishing up with lots of custard.

Bread & Butter Pudding

This yummy pudding is easy to make and a great way to use up any leftover hot cross buns or teacakes.

Ingredients

5 hot cross buns
50g butter
50g raisins
1 tin of custard (approx. 400g)
150ml milk
2 tbsp light brown sugar

Equipment

table knife
ovenproof dish
jug

1. Ask an adult to preheat the oven to 200°C/400°F/gas mark 6.

2. Slice the buns in half and butter each half.

3. Cut the buns into quarters and then arrange neatly in the bottom of an ovenproof dish, butter-side down. Sprinkle your raisins over the top.

4. Pour the custard into a jug, add the milk and stir together.

5. Pour the mixture over the buns, making sure they are completely covered. Sprinkle sugar over the top.

6. Ask an adult to put your pudding into the oven for 35 minutes, until the top is golden brown and crispy.

Sticky Toffee Pudding

This gooey dessert is perfect to warm
you up on a cold winter day.

Ingredients

175g dates, chopped
1 tsp baking soda
300ml boiling water
195g butter, room temperature,
   plus extra for greasing
170g caster sugar
2 eggs, beaten
225g plain flour
1 tsp baking powder
1 tsp vanilla essence
270g soft brown sugar
300ml double cream

Equipment

table knife, to chop the dates
2 bowls – 1 small, 1 large
fork, to beat the eggs
ovenproof dish
kitchen paper
wooden spoon
saucepan
jug

1. Put the dates and baking soda into a bowl. Ask an adult to pour over the boiling water. Soak for 1 hour.

2. Ask an adult to preheat the oven to 200°C/400°F/gas mark 6.

3. Use kitchen paper to grease the ovenproof dish with butter.

4. Put 70g of butter, all of the caster sugar, beaten eggs, flour, baking powder and vanilla essence into a bowl. Mix them together until you have a sloppy mixture. Stir in the dates and any leftover soaking water.

5. Spoon the mixture into the ovenproof dish. Ask an adult to put it into the oven for 40 minutes. Leave it to cool for 10 minutes.

6. For the sauce, put the remaining butter (125g), brown sugar and double cream into a saucepan and ask an adult to bring it to the boil for 3 minutes.

7. Pour the sauce into a jug and serve with the pudding.

TIP:
You can also serve your pudding with a dollop of vanilla ice cream for a bit of extra luxury.

Delicious Drinks

Easy-Peasy Lemon Fizz

When the weather is warm, all you need is a long cool drink. Try this recipe for hot summer days.

Ingredients

5 lemons
120g caster sugar
sparkling water

Equipment

table knife, to cut the lemons
jug
wooden spoon

1. Carefully cut each lemon in half and squeeze as much juice as you can from each piece into a large jug.

2. Measure out the caster sugar and tip it into the jug as well.

3. Stir with a long-handled spoon until there are no sugar granules left at the bottom.

4. Top up the jug with sparkling water and enjoy on a hot day!

Brilliant Berry Smoothie

Smoothies make a simple and tasty breakfast, but they're also great at any time of day.

Ingredients

100g strawberries
a banana
100g raspberries
100g plain yogurt
100g ice

Equipment

table knife, to cut the fruit
blender

WARNING! For this recipe, you'll need a blender. Make sure you ask an adult to help you.

1. Remove the stems from all the strawberries. Cut them in half and place in a blending jug.

2. Slice the banana, and add to the jug, along with the raspberries.

3. Tip in the yogurt, add the ice and blend until smooth. Make sure that the blender you're using will crush ice. If not, just chill your smoothie before drinking it. Delicious!

Banana Magic

Impress your friends and family with this mouth-watering smoothie recipe.

Ingredients

2 bananas
570ml (1-pint) milk
3–4 tbsp honey
a large handful of ice

Equipment

table knife, to cut the banana
blender

1. Peel the bananas and chop them into small slices.

2. Put the chopped bananas, milk, honey and ice into a blender and blend until smooth.

3. Pour into glasses and serve.

Strawberry Swirl

This pretty pink smoothie will always put
a smile on your face!

Ingredients

300g strawberries
(fresh or frozen)
500ml Greek yogurt
3–4 tbsp honey
a large handful of ice

Equipment

table knife, to cut the
strawberries
blender

1. If you are using fresh strawberries, slice off the stalks and
   chop the rest into a few smaller pieces (you don't have to
   worry about this if the strawberries are frozen).

2. Put the strawberries, yogurt, honey and ice into a blender
   and blend until smooth.

3. Pour into glasses and serve.

Index